DEFENDING THE DIGITAL PERIMETER

Empowering Your Human Firewall in Cybersecurity

D. L. Freeman

INTRODUCTION

Importance of the "Human Firewall" when Defending the Digital Perimeter in Cybersecurity

In today's interconnected world, organizations face an ever-expanding array of cyber threats that target their digital assets and sensitive information. Defending the digital perimeter refers to safeguarding the boundaries of an organization's network and systems against unauthorized access and cyberattacks. This proactive approach is crucial because cyber threats constantly evolve, and attackers are continuously seeking new ways to breach defenses. By defending the digital perimeter effectively, organizations can prevent data breaches, financial losses, and reputational damage.

The first line of defense against any cyberattack is the "Human Firewall". Businesses spend hundreds of thousands of dollars to recruit and hire the best employees to fill the roles in the organization. They pay for benefits, training for new skills, wage and salary, and the tools and technologies to enable the team to accomplish the goals and mission of the business plan.

Investing in the employees and the business requirements should also include significant time in training in the Human Firewall Concept. Employees need the training and tools to be empowered in the defense of cyber threats. This requires a top-down strategy where upper management is onboard and supports the initiative.

Many in the old school of thought think that the Information Technology Department is responsible for safeguarding the organization's data. They certainly play a major role in keeping the technology up to date, patched, as well as managing the network and user access.

However, every employee in the organization is a part of the Cybersecurity Team. This includes following all policies and procedures related to the use of technology and reporting any suspicious activity or incidents immediately. Physical access to the building is also part of cybersecurity. Employees should be trained to be aware of who is entering the building and verify the purpose for their visit. Larger businesses may have a visitor management system, but smaller ones may not.

Together with on-going training and cooperation with Management, the Technology Department, the Employee Group, and a Cyber Plan, the organization can safeguard the digital perimeter against cyber threats.

CONTENTS

Title Page

Copyright

Introduction

Chapter 1: The Human Firewall Concept

Chapter 2: Assessing the Current Security Landscape

Chapter 3: Establishing a Security-Conscious Culture

Chapter 4: Training and Education

Chapter 5: Reinforcing Strong Security Practices

Chapter 6: Building Effective Incident Response Capabilities

Chapter 7: Continuous Monitoring and Adaptation

Chapter 8: Collaboration and Partnerships

Chapter 9: Measurement and Improvement

Conclusion

Cybersecurity Resources

Books By This Author

About The Author

CHAPTER 1

The Human Firewall Concept

The human firewall is a powerful line of defense within an organization, consisting of its employees who interact with technology daily. They can act as both the first line of defense and the last line of protection against cyber threats. The human firewall concept recognizes that employees' knowledge, awareness, and actions play a critical role in cybersecurity. Empowering the human firewall involves educating employees about potential threats, training them on best practices, and fostering a security-conscious culture where every team member becomes a vigilant guardian of the digital perimeter.

In an increasingly interconnected digital landscape, the role of the human element in cybersecurity has become paramount. While advanced technologies and robust infrastructure provide critical layers of defense, the human factor remains the linchpin that can either fortify or weaken an organization's cybersecurity posture. The concept of the "human firewall" represents a paradigm shift in cybersecurity strategy, acknowledging that every employee can act as a strong line of defense against cyber threats. The human firewall plays a significant role in an organization's comprehensive cybersecurity plan.

The human firewall concept directly reduces the attack surface available to cybercriminals. Educated employees are less likely to fall for social engineering tactics such as phishing, spear phishing, and pretexting. By recognizing and thwarting these threats, employees become the first line of defense against data breaches and financial losses.

A vigilant human firewall contributes to early threat detection and rapid incident response. Employees who report anomalies or potential breaches enable timely mitigation, limiting the impact of attacks. This collaborative approach minimizes the dwell time of cyber threats and curtails their ability to inflict extensive damage.

To empower the human firewall, organizations must adopt a multifaceted and proactive cybersecurity approach. This involves assessing the current security landscape to understand potential weaknesses, building a security-conscious culture that encourages active participation, and providing comprehensive training and education to employees. By reinforcing strong security practices, establishing effective incident response capabilities, and continuously monitoring and adapting to emerging threats, organizations can create a resilient human firewall. Collaborative efforts and partnerships both within the organization and with external experts further strengthen the defense. Regular measurement and improvement ensure that cybersecurity measures evolve with the changing threat landscape, culminating in a fortified digital perimeter that protects against cyber threats effectively.

Real-World Examples Of The Human Firewall's Impact

Successful Defense: Morgan Stanley Phishing Attack Prevention

In 2019, Morgan Stanley, a global financial services firm, experienced a potential phishing attack targeting its employees. The firm's human firewall played a crucial role in preventing the attack from escalating. A suspicious email was sent to numerous employees, prompting them to click on a malicious link. However, employees were vigilant and immediately reported the suspicious email to the firm's IT security team. The team took swift action to block the malicious link, preventing any further spread of the phishing attempt.

Human Firewall Impact: Thanks to the proactive response of the human firewall, Morgan Stanley successfully averted a potential cyber incident, safeguarding sensitive financial data and maintaining customer trust.

Cost Savings: While the exact financial cost of potential damage was not publicly disclosed, a successful phishing attack could have led to severe financial losses, reputational damage, and legal implications for Morgan Stanley.

Successful Defense: Google Account Phishing Prevention

In 2017, Google experienced a sophisticated phishing attack targeting its employees. Attackers sent convincing phishing emails to employees, attempting to trick them into revealing their Google account credentials. However, Google's strong cybersecurity culture and human firewall proved effective. Many employees recognized the phishing attempt and reported it to the company's security team. The team promptly investigated and took steps to neutralize the threat, preventing unauthorized access to employee accounts and potential data breaches.

Human Firewall Impact: The heightened cybersecurity awareness and prompt reporting by Google employees played a pivotal role in thwarting the phishing attack.

Cost Savings: By preventing the attack from progressing, Google avoided potential data breaches, reputation damage, and financial losses associated with unauthorized access to employee accounts.

Successful Defense: IBM's Incident Response Team

IBM's incident response team is renowned for its effectiveness in mitigating cyber threats. In one instance, an employee received a suspicious email that appeared to be from a colleague. The email contained a link that, if clicked, would have installed malware on the recipient's computer. The vigilant employee recognized the sender's unusual email address and reported it to IBM's incident response team. The team promptly analyzed the email, identified it as a spear-phishing attempt, and disseminated an alert to other employees to raise awareness.

Human Firewall Impact: The employee's quick thinking and the incident response team's rapid action prevented potential malware infection and unauthorized access to IBM's network.

Cost Savings: By averting a potential cybersecurity incident, IBM avoided the costs associated with malware removal, data recovery, and potential business disruption.

Failure and Cost: Target Data Breach

In 2013, Target Corporation, a major US retail company, fell victim to a massive data breach that impacted approximately 41 million customer payment card accounts and exposed personal information of 70 million individuals. The breach originated from a successful phishing attack on a third-party HVAC vendor, which had access to Target's network. Attackers sent phishing emails to the vendor's employees, leading to the compromise of their login credentials. Once inside the vendor's system, the attackers leveraged their access to infiltrate Target's network, gaining unauthorized access to customer data.

Human Firewall Impact: The failure of the human firewall in the vendor's organization, which did not recognize the phishing attack, led to the initial breach.

Cost Incurred: The data breach resulted in significant financial losses for Target, including investigation costs, legal settlements, and a decline in customer trust. The company's estimated total cost of the breach was over $200 million.

Failure and Cost: Equifax Data Breach

In 2017, Equifax, one of the largest credit reporting agencies in the United States, suffered a massive data breach that exposed sensitive personal and financial information of approximately 147 million individuals. The breach was attributed to a vulnerability in Equifax's website software, which went unpatched. The failure to patch the vulnerability and secure the digital perimeter allowed attackers to gain access to the network and exfiltrate sensitive data over several months.

Human Firewall Impact: The lack of effective cybersecurity practices, including timely software patching, represented a failure of the human firewall in maintaining a secure digital environment.

Cost Incurred: The Equifax data breach resulted in substantial financial and reputational damage. Equifax faced legal settlements, regulatory fines, class-action lawsuits, and a significant erosion of consumer trust. The total cost of the breach was estimated to be over $1.38 billion.

These real-world examples highlight the critical role of the human firewall in cybersecurity. When employees are educated, vigilant, and proactive, they can prevent or mitigate potential cyber threats and significantly reduce the risk of costly security incidents. Conversely, when the human firewall is breached or fails, the organization can suffer severe financial and reputational consequences. It underscores the importance of investing in human-centric cybersecurity measures and creating a security-aware culture within organizations to strengthen the overall defense against cyber threats.

CHAPTER 2

Assessing The Current Security Landscape

Before fortifying the digital perimeter, it is essential to take stock of the existing cybersecurity measures in place. This involves assessing the effectiveness of firewalls, antivirus software, intrusion detection systems, and other security tools. The evaluation should identify any gaps or areas that may need improvement. Understanding the strengths and weaknesses of the current security infrastructure provides a foundation for making informed decisions to enhance overall cybersecurity.

Evaluating existing cybersecurity measures and their effectiveness is a crucial step in understanding the organization's security posture and identifying areas for improvement. Here are some practical examples of how to conduct such evaluations:

Penetration Testing (Pen Testing): Employ an external cybersecurity firm or an internal team to conduct controlled simulated cyberattacks against the organization's systems. Penetration testing identifies vulnerabilities and weaknesses in the infrastructure and applications. The results provide insights into potential entry points and areas that need stronger security measures.

Vulnerability Scanning: Use automated tools to scan the organization's network, servers, and applications for known vulnerabilities. Regular vulnerability scanning helps identify missing patches, outdated software, and misconfigurations that could be exploited by attackers.

Security Audits and Compliance Assessments: Conduct regular audits to assess the organization's compliance with industry standards and regulations. Evaluate adherence to cybersecurity policies and procedures and identify gaps in compliance that require attention.

Incident Response Tabletop Exercises: Organize tabletop exercises that simulate cyber incidents to assess the organization's incident response capabilities. These exercises help identify potential weaknesses in the response process, communication protocols, and coordination among teams.

User Awareness and Training Assessments: Conduct quizzes or surveys to gauge employees' knowledge of cybersecurity best practices. Assess how well employees recognize and respond to simulated phishing emails or other social engineering attempts.

Log Analysis and Monitoring: Review and analyze system logs, security event logs, and network activity to detect anomalous or suspicious behavior. Effective monitoring ensures timely detection and response to potential threats.

Red Team vs. Blue Team Exercises: Organize red team vs. blue team exercises where a "red team" tries to breach the organization's defenses, while the "blue team" defends and responds to the simulated attack. These exercises reveal gaps in the organization's security controls and incident response capabilities.

Business Impact Analysis (BIA): Conduct a BIA to identify critical assets and their dependencies. Understanding the potential impact of cyber incidents on key business processes helps prioritize security investments.

End-User Surveys and Feedback: Gather feedback from employees about their experiences with security measures, training programs, and the overall security culture. Employee insights can help identify areas where additional support or education is needed.

Comprehensive Security Metrics Dashboard: Develop a dashboard that consolidates relevant security metrics, such as the number of security incidents, response times, and the success of security awareness campaigns. This dashboard helps visualize the organization's security performance over time and facilitates data-driven decision-making.

By utilizing these practical evaluation methods, organizations can gain a better understanding of their cybersecurity effectiveness, identify weaknesses, and make informed decisions to improve their security posture. Continuous evaluation and improvement are essential to staying resilient against evolving cyber threats.

Identifying Vulnerabilities And Potential Entry Points

Cyber attackers often exploit vulnerabilities in systems and processes to gain unauthorized access. By conducting thorough vulnerability assessments, organizations can pinpoint potential entry points that attackers might target. Vulnerabilities can exist in software applications, network configurations, employee practices, or even physical access controls. Identifying these weak points allows organizations to prioritize remediation efforts and take proactive steps to close security gaps.

Performing a vulnerability assessment is a critical step in identifying and prioritizing security weaknesses within an organization's network, systems, and applications. Here's a practical step-by-step approach for conducting a vulnerability assessment.

Define the Scope and Objectives: Clearly define the scope of the vulnerability assessment, including the systems, applications, and network segments to be evaluated. Set specific objectives, such as identifying known vulnerabilities, assessing patch management, and prioritizing high-risk areas for remediation.

Select the Assessment Tools: Choose appropriate vulnerability scanning tools based on the organization's needs and budget. There are various commercial and open-source tools available, such as Nessus, OpenVAS, and Qualys, which can scan for known vulnerabilities in the network, servers, and applications.

Obtain Authorization and Coordinate with Stakeholders: Ensure that the vulnerability assessment is authorized and aligned with the organization's security policies. Coordinate with relevant stakeholders, including IT teams, system administrators, and business units, to schedule the assessment and minimize disruption to normal operations.

Perform the Vulnerability Scanning: Conduct the vulnerability scanning using the selected assessment tools. Scan all identified systems and applications within the defined scope. This process typically involves configuring the scanning tool with specific parameters and credentials to access the target systems.

Analyze the Results: Collect and analyze the scan results to identify vulnerabilities and potential risks. Prioritize the vulnerabilities based on severity ratings, potential impact, and exploitability. The assessment should categorize vulnerabilities as critical, high, medium, or low risk.

Verify and Validate Findings: To reduce false positives, manual verification and validation of identified vulnerabilities. This involves verifying whether the vulnerabilities are indeed exploitable and assessing their potential impact on the organization's assets and data.

Generate a Comprehensive Report: Prepare a detailed vulnerability assessment report that includes an executive summary, methodology, findings, and recommended actions. The report should be tailored for different audiences, such as technical teams and management.

Recommend Mitigation Strategies: Based on the identified vulnerabilities, recommend appropriate mitigation strategies and remediation actions. Provide guidance on patching, configuration changes, or additional security measures to address vulnerabilities.

Establish a Remediation Plan: Work with relevant stakeholders to create a remediation plan that prioritizes the most critical vulnerabilities for immediate action. Assign responsibility for each remediation task and set specific timelines for completion.

Monitor and Review Progress: Continuously monitor the progress of the remediation plan and review the effectiveness of the mitigation strategies. Regularly reassess the organization's security posture through periodic vulnerability assessments to ensure ongoing protection.

By following this practical approach, organizations can proactively identify and address vulnerabilities, reducing the risk of potential cyber incidents and improving their overall cybersecurity posture. Vulnerability assessments should be conducted regularly, ideally as part of a comprehensive cybersecurity program, to maintain a strong defense against emerging threats.

Understanding The Evolving Threat Landscape And Attack Vectors

The cyber threat landscape is dynamic and constantly changing. It is crucial to keep abreast of the latest threat intelligence and emerging attack vectors. Understanding how attackers operate and the tactics they use provides insight into the organization's potential exposure to specific threats. This knowledge helps security teams and employees stay vigilant and prepared to defend against the most relevant and current cyber threats. Regular threat intelligence updates ensure that the organization can adapt its defenses to stay ahead of evolving attack methods.

Keeping abreast of the latest threat intelligence and emerging attack vectors is crucial for organizations to stay ahead of cyber threats. Here's a practical approach to achieve this:

Subscribe to Threat Intelligence Feeds: Identify reputable threat intelligence providers and subscribe to their feeds. These providers regularly share updates on new and emerging threats, vulnerabilities, and attack techniques. Many cybersecurity vendors offer threat feeds that can be integrated into security information and event management (SIEM) systems for real-time analysis.

Join Information Sharing and Analysis Centers (ISACs): ISACs are industry-specific organizations that facilitate the sharing of cybersecurity threat information among their members. Joining relevant ISACs allows organizations to receive timely threat intelligence specific to their industry and collaborate with peers on threat mitigation strategies.

Participate in Cybersecurity Forums and Webinars: Attend cybersecurity forums, conferences, and webinars where experts and industry leaders discuss the latest threats and attack trends. These events often provide valuable insights into emerging attack vectors and best practices for defense.

Establish Relationships with Peers and Partners: Foster relationships with other organizations, both within the industry and across sectors. Collaborate with peers to share threat intelligence and experiences related to cyber incidents. Engaging in information-sharing partnerships can lead to a more comprehensive understanding of emerging threats.

Follow Security Research and Blogs: Keep track of security research and blogs from reputable cybersecurity experts and organizations. These resources often share in-depth analyses of recent cyberattacks, including tactics, techniques, and procedures used by threat actors.

Participate in Red Team Exercises: Organize or participate in red team exercises, where ethical hackers simulate real-world attacks against the organization's systems. Red team exercises provide firsthand experience of emerging attack techniques and potential vulnerabilities.

Collaborate with Managed Security Service Providers (MSSPs): Engage with MSSPs that offer threat intelligence services.

MSSPs can provide organizations with up-to-date information on emerging threats and offer guidance on enhancing security defenses.

Monitor Open-Source Intelligence (OSINT): Regularly monitor OSINT platforms, social media, and dark web sources for any chatter related to potential threats targeting the organization. This proactive approach helps identify potential risks early on.

Stay Informed on Security Vendor Updates: Keep track of security vendors' updates and advisories for their products and services. This includes patch releases, security bulletins, and best practice recommendations.

Continuous Training and Awareness: Invest in continuous cybersecurity training for employees to keep them updated on the latest threats and attack vectors. Educated and aware employees are better equipped to detect and respond to potential cyber threats.

By following this practical approach, organizations can proactively gather and analyze threat intelligence, gaining valuable insights into potential risks and exposure to emerging threats. This knowledge enables them to adapt their cybersecurity defenses and stay resilient against evolving cyber threats.

In summary, assessing the current security landscape involves evaluating existing security measures, identifying vulnerabilities, and staying informed about the ever-changing cyber threat landscape. This information forms the basis for developing a targeted and effective approach to empower the human firewall and fortify the digital perimeter against potential cyber threats.

CHAPTER 3

Establishing A Security-Conscious Culture

Educating Employees on The Importance of Cybersecurity

Building a security-conscious culture starts with ensuring that all employees understand the significance of cybersecurity. This involves clear and straightforward communication about the potential risks and consequences of cyber threats. Employees should be informed about the role they play in defending the organization's digital assets and protecting sensitive information. By raising awareness, employees are more likely to take security seriously and become proactive participants in the organization's cybersecurity efforts.

The best method to educate employees on the importance of cybersecurity involves a multi-faceted approach that is engaging, relevant, and ongoing. Here are some effective methods to achieve this:

Interactive Training Sessions: Conduct interactive cybersecurity training sessions that include real-world examples and scenarios relevant to employees' roles. Use multimedia presentations, videos, and quizzes to keep employees engaged and reinforce key concepts.

Simulated Phishing Exercises: Conduct simulated phishing exercises to raise awareness about the dangers of phishing attacks. Send mock phishing emails to employees and provide immediate feedback on their responses. These exercises help employees recognize phishing attempts and reinforce the importance of being vigilant with emails.

Gamified Learning: Gamification can be an effective way to make cybersecurity training enjoyable and memorable. Create cybersecurity-related games or quizzes with rewards and recognition for employees who actively participate and perform well.

Security Awareness Campaigns: Launch regular security awareness campaigns that focus on specific cybersecurity topics or themes. Use posters, emails, and internal communication channels to share tips, best practices, and success stories related to cybersecurity.

Personalized Learning Paths: Tailor cybersecurity training to individual roles and responsibilities within the organization. Employees in different departments may have varying cybersecurity needs, so personalized learning paths ensure that training is relevant and applicable to each employee's job function. Often ,CEOs, CFOs, and HR roles are higher risk targets for phishing scams and cyber-attacks because of their access to sensitive information and finances.

Bring Your Own Device (BYOD) Awareness: If the organization allows BYOD, educate employees on the risks and best practices for using personal devices securely within the workplace environment.

Guest Speakers and Workshops: Bring in cybersecurity experts or external speakers to conduct workshops or talks on cybersecurity trends, threats, and best practices. These external perspectives can enhance employees' understanding and engagement.

Security Champions Program: Establish a security champions program where passionate and knowledgeable employees become cybersecurity advocates and ambassadors. These champions can help disseminate security information within their teams and provide peer support.

Phishing Reporting and Feedback: Encourage employees to report suspicious emails and incidents promptly. Provide positive feedback and recognition when employees report potential threats, creating a culture of open communication and proactive security practices.

Continuous Training and Updates: Cybersecurity threats evolve rapidly, so provide continuous training and updates to keep employees informed about the latest threats and defense strategies. Regularly reinforce the importance of cybersecurity in various communication channels.

Remember that educating employees on cybersecurity is an

ongoing process. Regularly assess the effectiveness of the training program, gather feedback from employees, and adapt the approach based on the organization's specific needs and cybersecurity challenges. A well-informed and security-aware workforce becomes a significant asset in strengthening the human firewall and defending against cyber threats effectively.

Fostering A Sense Of Ownership And Responsibility For Security

Empowering employees to feel a sense of ownership and responsibility for cybersecurity is key to developing a strong human firewall. When employees understand that they are an integral part of the defense against cyber threats, they are more inclined to adopt secure practices in their daily work routines. Encouraging a culture where everyone feels accountable for cybersecurity creates a collaborative and united approach to protecting the organization.

Empowering employees to feel a sense of ownership and responsibility for cybersecurity involves creating a culture that fosters accountability and encourages active participation in protecting the organization. In addition to the methods listed above, here are a few more examples:

Involve Employees in Decision Making: Include employees in discussions and decision-making processes related to cybersecurity. Seek their input on security policies, tools, and training programs. When employees feel their opinions are valued, they are more likely to take ownership of security initiatives.

Recognize and Reward Security-Conscious Behavior: Establish a recognition program that rewards employees for practicing good cybersecurity habits. Acknowledge and celebrate those who consistently adhere to security best practices and contribute to a secure work environment.

Set Security Goals: Collaborate with employees to set specific security goals that align with the organization's cybersecurity objectives. Regularly track progress, share achievements, and celebrate milestones as a team.

Lead by Example: Leadership plays a crucial role in setting the tone for a security-conscious culture. When leaders demonstrate a strong commitment to cybersecurity and actively participate in security initiatives, employees are more likely to follow suit.

By implementing these examples, organizations can foster a culture where employees feel a genuine sense of ownership and responsibility for cybersecurity. This collective commitment strengthens the human firewall, making the organization more resilient against cyber threats and promoting a security-conscious work environment.

Promoting Awareness And Vigilance In Identifying And Reporting Threats

Instilling a culture of awareness and vigilance is critical in spotting potential threats early on. Employees should be trained to recognize signs of suspicious activities, phishing attempts, or any unusual behavior that could indicate a cyber threat. By encouraging a "see something, say something" mindset, employees become active participants in incident detection and reporting. Timely reporting of potential threats enables the organization to respond swiftly and prevent or mitigate potential damages.

Promoting awareness and vigilance in identifying and reporting threats is essential to strengthening the human firewall within an organization. The following are the best ways to achieve this:

By implementing these strategies, organizations can create a security-conscious culture where employees are aware, vigilant, and proactive in identifying and reporting potential threats. This collective effort significantly enhances the organization's ability to detect and respond to cyber incidents promptly, reducing the potential impact of security breaches.

Encouraging A Collaborative And Proactive Approach To Security

Cybersecurity is a collective effort that involves all employees, regardless of their roles within the organization. Encouraging collaboration and communication between teams fosters a proactive and united front against cyber threats. Employees should be empowered to share security concerns, ask questions, and seek guidance without fear of judgment. By promoting open dialogue and collaboration, the organization becomes more resilient and better equipped to address cybersecurity challenges effectively.

Encouraging a collaborative and proactive approach to security is essential for building a strong human firewall within an organization. Here are the best ways to achieve this:

Promote a Culture of Open Communication: Foster an environment where employees feel comfortable sharing security concerns, asking questions, and reporting potential threats. Encourage open communication across teams and departments to facilitate collaboration on security matters.

Cross-Departmental Collaboration: Facilitate cross-departmental collaboration on security initiatives. Encourage regular meetings or workshops where representatives from different teams can share insights, challenges, and best practices related to cybersecurity.

Shared Goals and Objectives: Align security objectives with broader organizational goals. Help employees understand how their proactive approach to security directly contributes to the overall success and resilience of the organization.

Encourage Knowledge Sharing: Organize knowledge-sharing sessions, lunch-and-learns, or webinars where employees can share their experiences with security incidents, threat trends, and successful defense strategies.

Incentives for Proactive Security: Implement a rewards system that recognizes and incentivizes proactive security behavior. Celebrate employees who actively contribute to improving the organization's security posture.

Encourage Collaboration During Incidents: During security incidents or breaches, foster a collaborative response approach. Involve relevant stakeholders from different teams to work together to identify the root cause, contain the threat, and implement necessary remediation.

Provide Access to Resources: Ensure that employees have access to relevant security resources, such as cybersecurity knowledge bases, best practice guidelines, and training materials. Easy access to resources encourages self-learning and proactive engagement.

Celebrate Collaborative Success: When cross-departmental collaboration leads to improved security outcomes or proactive threat mitigation, celebrate these successes openly. Recognition reinforces the importance of collaboration and encourages further engagement.

By adopting these strategies, organizations can create a culture of collaboration and proactive engagement in cybersecurity. Employees will feel empowered to take ownership of security and work together to strengthen the organization's defense against cyber threats. A collaborative approach ensures that the human firewall is strong and unified in its efforts to protect the organization's digital assets and sensitive information.

In summary, establishing a security-conscious culture involves educating employees about cybersecurity, fostering a sense of ownership and responsibility, promoting awareness and vigilance, and encouraging collaboration and proactive engagement. This culture empowers the human firewall, creating a workforce that is vigilant, proactive, and committed to safeguarding the digital perimeter against potential cyber threats.

CHAPTER 4

Training And Education

Providing Comprehensive Cybersecurity Training Programs

Comprehensive cybersecurity training equips employees with the knowledge and skills needed to defend against cyber threats effectively. This training should cover a wide range of topics, from basic security concepts to more advanced threat detection and incident response techniques. By offering regular and relevant training sessions, employees can stay up to date with the latest cybersecurity practices and technologies.

Introducing Employees To Common Threats And Attack Techniques

Employees need to be familiar with the various types of cyber threats they may encounter in their daily work. By educating them about common threats, such as phishing, malware, and social engineering, they can recognize the warning signs and avoid falling victim to these attacks. Real-world examples and simulations can help make the training engaging and practical.

Enhancing Knowledge Of Cybersecurity Best Practices

Cybersecurity best practices are essential guidelines that help employees protect themselves and the organization from potential risks. These practices may include using strong passwords, avoiding public Wi-Fi networks, and being cautious with email attachments. Reinforcing these practices through training ensures that employees develop good security habits in their day-to-day activities.

Offering Specialized Training On Social Engineering, Phishing, And Malware Defense

Specialized training on specific threat vectors, such as social engineering, phishing, and malware defense, provides employees with targeted knowledge and skills to counter these threats. By understanding the tactics used by attackers and learning effective defense strategies, employees become more capable of identifying and thwarting cyber-attacks.

A comprehensive cybersecurity training program is a structured and well-planned initiative that aims to educate all employees about cybersecurity best practices, potential threats, and their role in defending the organization against cyber-attacks. Here's an outline of a comprehensive cybersecurity training program.

Assessment and Needs Analysis: Conduct an initial assessment to understand the organization's current cybersecurity knowledge and identify areas that need improvement. Determine the specific cybersecurity training needs for different employee roles and departments.

Goal Setting and Objectives: Define clear goals and objectives for the training program, such as reducing the risk of security incidents, improving incident response, and fostering a security-conscious culture.

Curriculum Development: Develop a comprehensive curriculum that covers a wide range of cybersecurity topics, tailored to the needs of different employee groups. Include fundamental concepts, such as password security, social engineering awareness, phishing detection, data protection, and safe internet usage.

Delivery Methods: Utilize a mix of training delivery methods, including instructor-led sessions, e-learning modules, videos, gamified learning, and interactive workshops. Use real-world examples and simulations to make the training engaging and practical.

Role-Based Training: Provide role-based training to address specific security responsibilities and challenges faced by employees in different departments, such as IT, finance, HR, etc.

Phishing Awareness and Simulations: Conduct regular phishing awareness training and simulations to help employees recognize and respond to phishing attempts effectively.

Security Policies and Procedures: Educate employees about the organization's cybersecurity policies, procedures, and acceptable use guidelines. Emphasize the importance of complying with these policies to protect sensitive data and information.

Incident Response Training: Train employees on the proper procedures for reporting security incidents and the role they play in the incident response process.

Security Culture and Awareness: Promote a security-conscious culture by emphasizing that cybersecurity is everyone's responsibility. Encourage employees to actively participate in security initiatives and report any security concerns.

Measuring and Assessing Training Effectiveness: Continuously assess the effectiveness of the training program through quizzes, assessments, and feedback surveys. Use the results to identify areas for improvement and adjust the training as needed.

Continuous Education and Updates: Provide ongoing education and updates to keep employees informed about the latest cybersecurity threats and defense strategies. Reinforce training periodically to ensure that knowledge is retained and applied in daily work practices.

Senior Leadership Involvement: Engage senior leadership in the cybersecurity training program to demonstrate their commitment to security and set an example for all employees.

A comprehensive cybersecurity training program should be an ongoing initiative, regularly updated to reflect the evolving threat landscape and the organization's specific needs. It should empower employees with the knowledge and skills to become active defenders of the organization's digital assets, contributing to a more robust human firewall.

In summary, training and education play a crucial role in empowering the human firewall. Comprehensive cybersecurity training programs introduce employees to common threats and best practices, enhancing their knowledge and awareness. Specialized training on specific threats equips them with the necessary tools to defend against social engineering, phishing, and malware attacks. This well-rounded education ensures that employees are well-prepared to actively contribute to the organization's cybersecurity efforts.

CHAPTER 5

Reinforcing Strong Security Practices

Implementing Strong Password Policies and Multi-Factor Authentication

Passwords are the first line of defense against unauthorized access. Implementing strong password policies, such as using complex passwords, regularly updating them, and prohibiting password reuse, reinforces the importance of safeguarding accounts. Additionally, encourage the use of multi-factor authentication (MFA) to add an extra layer of protection, making it significantly harder for attackers to compromise accounts.

Promoting Secure Browsing Habits and Safe Online Practices

Safe online practices are essential for protecting against various cyber threats, including phishing and malware. Promote secure browsing habits, such as verifying website authenticity, avoiding suspicious links, and refraining from downloading files from untrusted sources. Teach employees about the dangers of public Wi-Fi and the importance of using a virtual private network (VPN) when accessing sensitive information remotely.

Emphasizing the Importance of Regular Software Updates and Patching

Regularly updating software and applying security patches are critical to addressing known vulnerabilities. Emphasize the significance of keeping operating systems, applications, and security software up to date to minimize the risk of exploitation by cyber attackers. Automating software updates can streamline the process and ensure a more secure environment.

Encouraging Secure Remote Work Practices and Protection of Personal Devices

As remote work becomes increasingly prevalent, it's crucial to promote secure remote work practices. Educate employees about the risks associated with using personal devices for work-related tasks and provide guidance on securing personal devices, such as enabling screen locks, using encryption, and setting up remote wipe capabilities. Encourage employees to connect to the company's network via secure virtual private networks (VPNs) when working remotely.

By implementing these practices and continually reinforcing their importance, organizations empower employees to become active participants in their cybersecurity defenses. A security-conscious workforce is more vigilant in detecting potential threats and taking proactive measures to protect sensitive data and digital assets. Ultimately, a proactive approach to reinforcing strong security practices helps maintain a resilient and secure work environment.

CHAPTER 6

Building Effective Incident Response Capabilities

Incident response plans are crucial in outlining the steps to be taken in the event of a cybersecurity incident. Work with relevant teams, including IT, security, legal, and communications, to develop comprehensive incident response plans tailored to different types of incidents. These plans should define roles and responsibilities, incident categorization, containment strategies, and recovery steps.

A well-structured cybersecurity incident response plan is crucial for effectively managing and mitigating the impact of security incidents. Here are the key components that should be included in a comprehensive incident response plan.

Developing Incident Response Plans and Procedures

Roles and Responsibilities: Define and document the roles and responsibilities of individuals and teams involved in the incident response process. This includes incident response team members, communication coordinators, legal advisors, and senior management.

Incident Categorization and Severity Levels: Develop a clear framework for categorizing incidents based on their severity and potential impact. Assign severity levels to different types of incidents to prioritize the response and allocate resources appropriately.

Incident Reporting and Escalation: Establish procedures for how incidents should be reported, who should be notified, and the appropriate escalation paths. Define communication channels and contact information for incident reporting.

Communication Plan: Outline a communication plan for both internal and external stakeholders. Define who should be informed, how updates will be communicated, and the messaging to be shared during different stages of the incident.

Containment and Eradication: Describe the steps to isolate and contain the incident to prevent further damage. Provide guidance on identifying the source of the incident, removing malicious elements, and restoring affected systems to a secure state.

Evidence Collection and Preservation: Detail procedures for collecting and preserving evidence related to the incident. This may include network logs, system snapshots, emails, and any other relevant data that could aid in understanding the scope and impact of the incident.

Forensics and Analysis: Define processes for conducting a thorough analysis of the incident. This involves identifying the attack vector, understanding the tactics used by the attacker, and assessing the extent of data compromise.

Notification and Legal Requirements: Outline requirements for legal notifications, such as breach notification laws and regulations that may apply to the incident. Include procedures for engaging legal counsel and regulatory authorities as needed.

Recovery and Remediation: Describe the steps for restoring affected systems, data, and services to normal operation. Provide guidance on validating the effectiveness of remediation efforts and monitoring for any residual threats.

Lessons Learned and Post-Incident Review: Emphasize the importance of conducting a thorough review after the incident is resolved. Document lessons learned, identify areas for improvement, and update the incident response plan based on the insights gained.

Training and Awareness: Include ongoing training and awareness initiatives to ensure that employees are informed about the incident response plan, their roles, and the importance of reporting incidents promptly.

Testing and Drills: Describe how the incident response plan will be tested through regular tabletop exercises and simulated incident scenarios. These drills help validate the effectiveness of the plan and identify areas that need improvement.

Document Retention and Disposal: Define how incident-related documentation will be retained and securely stored for compliance and future reference. Outline procedures for the proper disposal of sensitive incident data.

A well-constructed incident response plan provides a structured and organized approach to addressing cybersecurity incidents, minimizing their impact, and facilitating a coordinated response across the organization. Regular updates and continuous improvement ensure that the plan remains effective in the face of evolving cyber threats.

Training Employees on Incident Detection and Reporting

Educate employees on the signs of a potential security incident, such as unusual system behavior, unauthorized access attempts, or suspicious emails. Provide clear guidance on how and where to report incidents promptly. Encourage employees to report any security-related concerns promptly, fostering a proactive incident reporting culture.

Establishing Communication Channels and Escalation Processes

Effective communication is vital during a cybersecurity incident. Establish communication channels that enable seamless information sharing among incident response teams. Define escalation processes to ensure that incidents are appropriately escalated to higher management or external authorities when required.

Conducting Regular Incident Response Drills and Exercises

Practice makes perfect. Conduct regular incident response drills and exercises, such as tabletop simulations or red team vs. blue team exercises, to test the organization's incident response capabilities. These exercises help identify areas for improvement, validate response plans, and enhance coordination among different teams.

By building effective incident response capabilities, organizations can significantly reduce the impact of cybersecurity incidents and minimize downtime. The ability to detect, contain, and respond to incidents promptly ensures that security breaches are swiftly addressed, maintaining the trust of customers, partners, and stakeholders. Additionally, a well-prepared incident response team contributes to a faster recovery and reduces the financial and reputational damage caused by cyber incidents.

CHAPTER 7

Continuous Monitoring And Adaptation

Implementing Security Monitoring Systems and Technologies

Continuous monitoring involves deploying security systems and technologies that actively track and analyze network activities and data access. These systems can detect potential threats and anomalies in real-time, allowing swift action to be taken in response to emerging cyber threats. By having a constant watch over the digital perimeter, organizations can identify and address security incidents before they escalate.

Analyzing Security Metrics and Indicators for Proactive Detection

Security metrics provide valuable insights into the organization's security posture. By regularly analyzing key indicators, such as the number of attempted breaches, successful intrusions, and incident response times, security teams can proactively identify areas that may require additional attention or improvements. Data-driven analysis enables the organization to respond effectively to emerging threats and continuously optimize its cybersecurity strategies.

Staying Updated on Emerging Threats and Evolving Attack Techniques

The cyber threat landscape is dynamic and constantly evolving. Staying informed about the latest threats and attack techniques is essential to maintaining an effective defense. Security teams should actively monitor threat intelligence sources and collaborate with industry peers to share information. Being aware of emerging threats allows the organization to adapt its security measures promptly and effectively.

Adapting Security Measures and Training Programs Accordingly

As cyber threats evolve, so should the organization's cybersecurity measures and training programs. Continuous monitoring and analysis help identify areas of improvement and potential vulnerabilities. By adapting security measures, implementing new technologies, and refining training approaches, the organization ensures that its defenses remain resilient and effective against the latest threats.

In summary, continuous monitoring and adaptation are essential for maintaining a robust cybersecurity defense. By implementing security monitoring systems, analyzing security metrics, and staying informed about emerging threats, organizations can proactively detect and respond to potential cyber threats. Adapting security measures and training programs based on insights and evolving threat landscapes ensures that the human firewall remains equipped to defend the digital perimeter effectively.

CHAPTER 8

Collaboration And Partnerships

Engaging Employees as Active Participants in Cybersecurity Defense

Effective cybersecurity defense is a team effort that involves everyone within the organization. Engaging employees as active participants in the defense strategy strengthens the human firewall. Encourage open communication and feedback to create a sense of ownership and responsibility for cybersecurity. When employees feel valued and empowered in the process, they are more likely to be proactive in identifying and reporting potential threats.

Encouraging Cross-Departmental Collaboration on Security Initiatives

Cybersecurity is not limited to the IT department; it involves various teams and departments across the organization. Encourage collaboration and cooperation between different departments to ensure that cybersecurity practices are integrated into every aspect of the organization's operations. By working together, teams can share insights and expertise, leading to a more robust and comprehensive cybersecurity strategy.

Building Partnerships with External Experts and Industry Peers

Cybersecurity is a constantly evolving field, and no organization can do it all alone. Building partnerships with external cybersecurity experts, consultants, or industry peers can provide valuable insights, best practices, and knowledge sharing. Leveraging external expertise ensures that the organization benefits from the collective knowledge of the cybersecurity community.

Sharing Best Practices and Lessons Learned for Collective Defense

Knowledge sharing is crucial in the fight against cyber threats. Encourage the sharing of best practices and lessons learned within the organization and with other industry peers. By sharing experiences and strategies, organizations can collectively improve their defenses against common cyber threats. Collaborative learning ensures that everyone is better equipped to face emerging challenges.

In summary, collaboration and partnerships are vital for a strong and resilient cybersecurity defense. Engaging employees as active participants, encouraging cross-departmental cooperation, and building external partnerships create a collaborative approach to security. Sharing best practices and lessons learned enables organizations to benefit from collective knowledge, strengthening the human firewall and the organization's overall cybersecurity posture.

CHAPTER 9

Measurement And Improvement

Establishing Key Performance Indicators (Kpis) for Security Effectiveness

Key performance indicators (Kpis) are measurable metrics that help gauge the effectiveness of the organization's cybersecurity efforts. By defining relevant Kpis, such as incident response times, successful threat mitigations, and employee training completion rates, the organization can assess its security posture and identify areas that need improvement. Kpis serve as benchmarks for measuring progress over time and ensuring that cybersecurity goals are being met.

DEFENDING THE DIGITAL PERIMETER

Conducting Regular Assessments and Audits of Security Practices

Regular assessments and audits are essential for evaluating the organization's adherence to cybersecurity policies and best practices. These evaluations provide a comprehensive view of the effectiveness of security measures and identify potential vulnerabilities or areas of non-compliance. Conducting these assessments on a scheduled basis ensures that the organization stays proactive in its security efforts.

Gathering Employee Feedback and Suggestions for Improvement

Employees are on the front lines of cybersecurity defense and can offer valuable insights into the effectiveness of security measures. Gathering feedback from employees about their experiences, challenges, and suggestions for improvement creates a culture of continuous improvement. Employees may provide valuable input that can lead to enhanced security practices and a stronger human firewall.

Continuously Iterating and Enhancing Security Measures Based on Data-Driven Insights

Data-driven insights from assessments, audits, and employee

feedback serve as the foundation for continuous improvement. Using this data, the organization can identify patterns, trends, and areas for enhancement. Continuously iterating and enhancing security measures based on these insights ensures that the organization remains agile and adaptable in the face of evolving cyber threats.

In summary, measurement and improvement are essential for maintaining an effective cybersecurity defense. Establishing relevant KPIs, conducting regular assessments, and gathering employee feedback provide valuable data for evaluating security effectiveness. Based on this information, the organization can continuously iterate and improve its security measures, ensuring that the human firewall remains strong, and the digital perimeter is fortified against cyber threats.

CONCLUSION

Recap Of The Key Elements In Defending The Digital Perimeter

Defending the digital perimeter is a multifaceted endeavor that involves empowering the human firewall and implementing robust cybersecurity measures. Throughout this process, several key elements contribute to a comprehensive defense strategy.

Implementing Robust Cybersecurity Measures

Firewalls and Intrusion Detection/Prevention Systems: These network security tools act as the first line of defense, monitoring and controlling incoming and outgoing network traffic. They block potentially malicious traffic and intrusions.

Importance: Firewalls and intrusion prevention systems protect against external threats, such as hacking attempts or malware downloads. For example, if a hacker tries to exploit a vulnerability in the company's web server, the firewall can block the attacker's IP address.

Endpoint Security: Endpoint security solutions safeguard individual devices (e.g., computers, mobile devices) from threats. They include antivirus software, host-based intrusion detection systems, and encryption tools.

**Importance*: In the event that an employee's laptop becomes infected with malware, endpoint security can detect and quarantine the threat, preventing it from spreading to other devices or compromising sensitive data.

Access Controls and Authentication: Properly configured access controls and strong authentication mechanisms ensure that only authorized users can access specific systems and data.

**Importance*: Access controls and authentication prevent unauthorized access to critical systems and data. For instance, multi-factor authentication (MFA) requires users to provide two or more authentication factors, enhancing security. Without MFA, a stolen password alone could lead to a breach.

Patch Management: Regularly updating software and systems with security patches is essential for addressing known vulnerabilities. Unpatched systems are prime targets for attackers.

◆ ◆ ◆

Importance: Without effective patch management, organizations remain vulnerable to known exploits. The WannaCry ransomware attack in 2017, which impacted unpatched Windows systems, exemplifies the consequences of neglecting patching.

◆ ◆ ◆

Incident Response Plan: Having a well-defined incident response plan in place is critical for efficiently addressing security incidents when they occur. It outlines the steps to take in the event of a breach, from detection to recovery.

Importance: An incident response plan ensures that the organization can respond quickly and effectively to minimize damage. In the case of a data breach, a well-executed response can limit data exposure and reputational harm.

In conclusion, defending the digital perimeter is a multifaceted effort that combines the strength of the human firewall with robust cybersecurity measures. Empowering employees through training and fostering a security-conscious culture is as vital as implementing technical defenses. Together, these elements create a comprehensive defense strategy that mitigates risk and safeguards an organization's digital assets.

Key Takeaways

Empowering your human firewall in the organization is essential for enhancing cybersecurity awareness and resilience. Here are the key takeaways from this approach:

Active Defense: Employees are not just end-users but active defenders against cyber threats. Their vigilance and knowledge play a crucial role in preventing and mitigating security incidents.

Shared Responsibility: Cybersecurity is a shared responsibility that extends to every employee. Fostering this mindset promotes a collective effort to protect sensitive data and digital assets.

Threat Detection: Empowered employees are better at recognizing and reporting suspicious activities, potential threats, and policy violations. This early detection is critical for swift incident response.

Prevention of Social Engineering: Training and awareness help employees identify and resist social engineering tactics such as phishing, spear-phishing, and pretexting, which are often used by attackers.

Reduced Attack Surface: A well-informed workforce reduces the attack surface by minimizing the success rate of social engineering attacks and other human-centric vulnerabilities.

Incident Response Improvement: Empowered employees contribute to a more effective incident response by providing early warnings and valuable insights into the nature of threats.

Cultural Transformation: Fostering a security-conscious culture extends beyond the workplace and encourages secure behavior in employees' personal lives, enhancing overall cybersecurity resilience.

Risk Mitigation: By investing in cybersecurity education and awareness, organizations mitigate the risk of data breaches, financial losses, and reputational damage.

Continuous Training: Cybersecurity awareness should be an ongoing process with regular updates and refresher courses to keep employees informed about evolving threats.

Compliance and Regulation: Meeting cybersecurity compliance requirements becomes more achievable when employees are aware of their responsibilities and the importance of adhering to security policies.

Collaboration: Empowered employees are more likely to collaborate effectively with IT and security teams, facilitating a coordinated response to incidents.

Cost Savings: A vigilant workforce helps prevent costly security incidents, such as data breaches, which can result in substantial financial losses and legal liabilities.

Adaptability: Empowered employees are better equipped to adapt to new and emerging cybersecurity challenges, making the organization more resilient to evolving threats.

Positive Reinforcement: Recognition and incentives for security-conscious behavior motivate employees to actively participate in cybersecurity efforts.

Continuous Improvement: Regular assessment of training programs, incident response drills, and updates to security policies ensure that the human firewall remains strong and adaptable.

In summary, empowering the human firewall in your

organization is a proactive strategy that strengthens cybersecurity resilience by making every employee an active participant in defending against cyber threats. This approach fosters a culture of security consciousness and shared responsibility, ultimately reducing the organization's risk exposure and enhancing its ability to respond effectively to security incidents.

Reinforcement Of The Importance Of Empowering The Human Firewall

The human firewall is a critical aspect of cybersecurity defense. By educating and engaging employees, fostering a security-conscious culture, and providing continuous training, organizations empower their workforce to be active defenders against cyber threats.

Call To Action For Organizations To Prioritize And Invest In Human-Centric Cybersecurity

Cyber threats are ever evolving, and the human element remains a vital component of a strong defense. Organizations must recognize the importance of investing in human-centric cybersecurity. By prioritizing cybersecurity training and education, fostering a collaborative environment, and continuously improving security measures, organizations can enhance their resilience against cyber threats and protect their digital assets effectively.

In summary, defending the digital perimeter is a collective effort that involves empowering the human firewall through education, collaboration, and continuous improvement. By prioritizing cybersecurity and recognizing the significance of the human element, organizations can create a robust defense against the ever-changing landscape of cyber threats. Together, employees and technology form an interconnected defense that safeguards the organization's digital perimeter and secures its most valuable assets.

This book provides a general framework for defending the digital perimeter by empowering the human firewall. Depending on the specific context and requirements of the organization, additional elements and requirements may be needed for compliance within specific industries or business needs.

Dear Reader,

Thank you for reading, *Defending The Digital Perimeter: Empowereing Your Human Firewall in Cybersecurity*. I hope you have gained some insights and tools related to The Human Firewall Concept as it relates to the overall scheme of Cybersecurity. An honest review would help other readers when considering this book.

Thanks again,

D. L. Freeman

CYBERSECURITY RESOURCES

Cybersecurity Organizations And Websites:

National Institute of Standards and Technology (NIST): https://www.nist.gov/cybersecurity

Cybersecurity and Infrastructure Security Agency (CISA): https://www.cisa.gov/cybersecurity

Security Blogs And News Sources:

Krebs on Security: https://krebsonsecurity.com/

The Hacker News: https://thehackernews.com/

Dark Reading: https://www.darkreading.com/

Threatpost: https://threatpost.com/

Infosecurity Magazine:https://www.infosecurity-magazine.com/news/

National Cybersecurity Alliance - https://staysafeonline.org/resources/

Cybersecurity & Infrastructure Security Agency - Weekly Vulnerability Bulletins - https://www.cisa.gov/news-events/bulletins

Security Standards And Best Practices:

NIST Cybersecurity Framework: https://www.nist.gov/cyberframework

Please note that the inclusion of specific resources and tools does not imply endorsement or guarantee of their effectiveness. It is always recommended to conduct your own research and evaluation before using any tools or services.

Employee Cybersecurity Training:

SANS Securing the Human: SANS Securing the Human offers a variety of cybersecurity training programs and resources specifically designed for employees. They provide interactive training modules, videos, newsletters, and posters to raise awareness and educate employees about cybersecurity best practices. Website: https://www.sans.org/security-awareness-training

KnowBe4: KnowBe4 is a popular security awareness training platform that offers a wide range of interactive training modules, simulated phishing campaigns, and security awareness resources. They provide customizable training programs to suit different organizational needs. Website: https://www.knowbe4.com/

PhishMe: PhishMe, now part of Cofense, provides phishing simulation and training solutions. They offer interactive training modules, phishing email templates, and reporting tools to help organizations train employees to recognize and respond to phishing attacks. Website: https://cofense.com/

InfoSec Institute: InfoSec Institute offers cybersecurity training courses, including employee awareness training. They cover topics such as social engineering, phishing, password security, and secure email practices. Website: https://www.infosecinstitute.com/

Security Mentor: Security Mentor provides a comprehensive library of online security awareness training courses. They offer engaging, interactive modules on various cybersecurity topics, including secure computing, mobile device security, and safe web browsing. Website: https://www.securitymentor.com/

National Cyber Security Centre (NCSC): The NCSC offers free cybersecurity training resources and guidance for businesses and employees. They provide e-learning modules, toolkits, and best practice guides to help organizations improve their security awareness. Website: https://www.ncsc.gov.uk/collection/training-resources

Cybrary: Cybrary is an online platform that offers a wide range of cybersecurity training courses, including courses suitable for employee training. They cover topics such as cybersecurity awareness, secure coding, and incident response. Website: https://www.cybrary.it/

Udemy: Udemy is an online learning platform that offers a variety of cybersecurity courses. They have courses designed for employees, covering topics like cybersecurity awareness, data protection, and secure communication. Website: https://www.udemy.com/

Remember, effective cybersecurity training should be an ongoing process. It is important to regularly reinforce and update training materials to keep up with emerging threats and evolving best practices. Additionally, consider customizing training programs to align with your organization's specific needs and risk profile.

BOOKS BY THIS AUTHOR

A Comprehensive Guide To Understanding Cybersecurity: Protecting Yourself In The Digital World

In this comprehensive book, we will explore the fundamentals of cybersecurity, the risks posed by cybercriminals, and the best practices to protect yourself from becoming a victim of cybercrime. From understanding the current state of cyber threats to implementing robust security measures, this guide aims to equip you with the knowledge and tools necessary to safeguard your digital life.

Whether you are a beginner looking to enhance your cybersecurity knowledge or an experienced user seeking a refresher, this book will cover essential topics such as password security, two-factor authentication (2FA), phishing email security, secure web browsing, mobile device security, and more. We will also delve into emerging cybersecurity trends and technologies shaping the digital landscape.

By the end of this book, you will have a solid foundation in cybersecurity practices, empowering you to navigate the digital world with confidence and protect your personal information from cyber threats. Remember, being proactive in cybersecurity is the key to staying safe online.

By implementing the best practices outlined in this book, staying informed about the latest threats and technologies, and fostering a culture of security awareness, you can significantly reduce the likelihood of falling victim to cyber-attacks.

ABOUT THE AUTHOR

D. L. Freeman

D. L. Freeman has spent more than twenty years of his career in the technology industry. He has worked for critical infrastructure organizations with a role of ensuring Reliability, Business Continuity, and Data Security.

He has directed and implemented Cybersecurity measures and best practices including, the education and training of employees.

He has had the privilege to work alongside multiple organizations and professionals in collaboration with the end goal of Cybersecurity Implementation and Awareness.

D. L. Freeman has spent his career in technology focusing on data security, integration, and innovation. He has worked in an industry that is tasked with maintaining, operating, and protecting critical infrastructure.
He has worked alongside multiple organizations and professionals in collaborative efforts to protect the data and critical assets with Comprehensive Cybersecurity Implementation and Training the "Human Firewall".

Cyber threats are ever evolving, and the human element remains a vital component of a strong defense. Organizations must recognize the importance of investing in human-centric cybersecurity.
The human firewall is a critical aspect of cybersecurity defense. By educating and engaging employees, fostering a security-conscious culture, and providing continuous training, organizations empower their workforce to be active defenders against cyber threats.

ISBN 9798861000574

9 798861 000574